Rosary of love

SUFI MYSTICISM

notionpress.com

Rosary of love

SUFI MYSTICISM

IKSHIT SATIJA

notionpress.com

Notion Press

Old No. 38, New No. 6
McNichols Road, Chetpet
Chennai - 600 031

First Published by Notion Press 2016

ISBN 978-93-86009-91-3

Message

It is very heartening to note that Shri Ikshit Satija who is a budding poet writes such soul-stirring poems. In these days of commercialization when the entire world seems to be running after the fleeting pleasures of the world it is a matter of great joy to come across someone who in spite of being so young is deeply interested in spiritual themes. The poems are of a deep spiritual fervour and are written in a beautiful and flowing style. I wish him all the best and pray to the Almighty to bless him with true spiritual insight.

Shantatmananda

Swami Shantatmananda

Secretary

Contents

1. The Wait....1
2. Death....2
3. Woeful Plight of the lover....3
4. Masterly Grace....4
5. Linguistic Limitations....5
6. The Divine Gift....6
7. The Path of Yearning....7
8. Eternity within a moment....8
9. Gifts on the Path....9
10. Transcendental Origins....10
11. The Divine King Maker....11
12. The Universal Paradox....12
13. Dignity of the Seeker....14
14. The Riddle of Love....16
15. Deja vu....17
16. The Mother Divine....19
17. To the Ultimate Godhead....20
18. Love's Strife....21
19. Eternal Life....22
20. Dissolution of the Ego....23
21. Glimpse of the Reality....24
22. Discovery of the Beloved....25
23. Divine Wine....26
24. Divine Visit....27
25. Beauty of Divinity....28
26. Spiritual Yearning....29
27. A Myth Called Death....30

28. Ecstatic Musings 31
29. A Dialogue with the Beloved 32
30. The Master 33
31. Divine Ennui 34
32. The Universal Delusion 35
33. Ephemeral Existence 36
34. Conquest of the Beloved 37
35. Divine Anxiety 38
36. Priceless Devotion 39
37. The Wordly Wizard 40
38. Literary Might 41
39. The Deadly Boon 42
40. Religion of Love 43
41. Descent of Divinity 44
42. The Divine Cowherd 45
43. The Saga of Vanity 47
44. The Night of Delight 49
45. Ruthless Violence and Musings in Silence 51
46. Counsel to the Mind 52
47. A Celebration Called Life 53
48. The Apparent Truth 54
49. Love's Reward 55
50. A Saga Called Life 56
51. The Mother Divine 57
52. The Universal Delusion 58
53. The Quest for Freedom 59
54. The Circus of the Mind 60
55. On Poetry 61
56. Fatal Love 62
57. Eternal Sojourn of the Mind 63
58. The Jewel Within 64
59. A Utopian Fantasy 65

60. Eternity of Life 66
61. Cosmic Worship 67
62. The Beatific Vision 68
63. Unspeakable Truth 69
64. Anguish of the Soul 70
65. The Spiritual Master 71
66. The Existential Crisis 72
67. Manacles of the Mind 73
68. Immaculate Love 74
69. Transformation of the Soul 75
70. Divine Anguish 76
71. Love's Paradox 77
72. Advise to the Mind 78
73. A Prayer to the Mother 79
74. Love for Writing 80
75. Inexplicable Bliss 81
76. Grace of the Master 82
77. God's Ungodly World 83
78. Karma-The Ultimate Retribution 84
79. Love: The Ultimate Obligation 85
80. Linguistic Frailties 86
81. Divine Bondage 87
82. The Wedding Supernal 88
83. Pain of Indifference 89
84. Religion of Love not Bondage 90
85. Poetry as Worship 91
86. Benedictions of Love 92
87. The Treasure Beyond Measure 93
88. Spiritual Evolution 94
89. Life is a dream 95
90. Creation of Love 96
91. A Relic Called Love 97

92. Ephemeral Pleasures....98
93. Puny Yet Grand.... 99
94. Cosmic Mother.... 100
95. Psychomachia....101
96. The Union with the Unknowable....102
97. Universal Mother of Endless Love....103
98. Beads of Divinity....104
99. Poetic Inspiration....106
100. Traversing the Mind....107
101. Divine Wine....108
102. Saga of the Master....109
103. The Enigma of Love....110
104. Entreaty to the Mother.... 111
105. The Cosmic Illusion.... 112
106. Death and its Trappings.... 113
107. Eternal Consciousness.... 114
108. Farewell.... 115

1

The Wait

Another year passes as I remain in solitary repast,
Waiting for the call of the Master I hope my body should last.
Countless days have passed and endless nights as well,
In my self-imposed exile there is none with me to tell;
My flights of the soul and tales of visitations divine,
With whom can I share these gifts of the Beloved that transcend space and time.
Let tears be the ornaments of my face,
And my hair be the rope by which I hold the Beloved in embrace.
Once if I behold Your mesmerising form,
All rituals shall drop and so each and every norm.
The most precious gift in the form of a family I have attained,
May they attain perennial bliss and fate never treat them with disdain.
A web of words I construe to catch the uncanny spider,
But verbosity is no excuse when it comes to feelings decipher.

2

Death

Death is the ultimate lullaby,
All that take birth are destined to die.
Like children in jest make castles of sand,
We intend to deceive death by every plan.
Only when It comes to stake its claim,
We realise that all of humanity is the same.
We are the debtors of this earth,
Wisdom lies in playing the game called life with mirth.
In this saga of life and death,
Let us embrace all that we met.
In this ephemeral play let us never forget,
For if joys are transitory then so is pain,
Why then must sorrow drive you insane?
Your lifetime is but a second in the whole cosmic saga,
Be awake before Death sings its deadly raga.

3

Woeful Plight of the lover

How can I comprehend Your ways my Mother,
My intellect is finite and in a spot of bother.
You command the Universe and hold it in Your sway,
I am but a minute worm caught in the labyrinth of Thy way.
I depend on You for every chore of mine,
By Thy Grace everything with me is divine.
Thy love is so sacred and pristine,
I have felt it in the waking state as well as in dream.
My Love for You increases every hour,
Love alone can bind You such is its power.
May my heart ever sing of Thy love,
The panacea for all ills and it is also a treasure trove.

4

Masterly Grace

I seek you afar when thou art near,
Till you are enshrined in my heart there is no fear.
Infect you did with a single glance my soul,
And made divine longing my only goal.
Strange appear to me the customs of this world,
Vain are its values to the soul which is a migratory bird.
A play of a few days is this life,
Why make it a veritable hell of strife?
The self knows you to be my only goal,
I have sought you through births untold.
I came from a realm which transcended all at thy behest,
Without seeing you my soul can never find rest.
Give me once more thy precious glance,
Whether in the state of waking or that of trance.
Separation from you is the infernal fire that consumes my soul,
When shall such a day arrive that my eyes shall you behold.

5

Linguistic Limitations

In the labyrinth of the mind,
I wander so as you to find.
Within a single moment lies eternity for the lover,
This union of the Heart is for the Self to discover.
In Thy absence is Your presence palpable,
Where language ends begins malleable.
Utter stillness pervades my Being,
Yet You O Beloved remain still unseen.
For the sake of Thy Love I wander like a ministrel,
Now comes a stage whence the difference between us none can tell.
Losing my Self I have gained Thee,
Let the world dissolve for it is nothing but a shadow for me.

6

The Divine Gift

A debt that I can't repay,
Of love eternal here to stay.
The Divine who comes as mother,
A reflection of affection on a feather.
A conduit of love supramental,
Yet appearing as human with no mantle.
No pretensions of the outer garb,
Yet of love never debarred.
I thank you for being the polestar,
Being distant yet never afar.
Contradictions arrive when I articulate in words,
Thy dovelike purity incomparable with another bird.`

7

The Path of Yearning

Let Love take its course,
My agony from this malady is not a hoax.
It is difficult for the world to glimpse my pain,
In pursuit of the Beloved I have turned insane.
This infectious glance from the Great Master has ruined my life,
I am ostracized from the society and have taken misery as my wife.
To the worldly wise I have no words to explain,
For my longing transcends language and from reason does abstain.
No longer will I care for the prattle of fools,
For man invented language and reason to betray Reality but never to employ them as effective tools.

8

Eternity within a moment

Love eternal I seek of the Soul,
A bond worth its weight in gold.
Yet priceless is the companionship I so earnestly seek,
Granted by the Sovereign to the meek.
I will barter this world and the next,
To obtain the gem of Thy affection before which all desires are jest.
Earthly beings marred by defects in plenty,
Are not to be included in my gentry.
The people of the world show their apparent love,
To gratify their own sense up and above.
Absolved of all primitive desires,
I kindle within my being the Divine Fire.
Let my heart yearn alone for Thee,
Indifferent to the play of the world appearing real though transitory.

9

Gifts on the Path

Now each moment is ecstatic immersed in perennial delight,
My soul sings of the love it has for the One with boundless might.
My days whirl like the Sufis of yore,
While nights are with the Beloved who of transcendental bliss is the store.
Finally my love bears fruit with the golden dawn,
The tears and lamentations that adorned my person are now forlorn.
May my life be a prayer unto Thee,
What else can I offer having forgotten in love even 'me'?

10

Transcendental Origins

On this day what I can desire?
My being, my very soul is on fire.
The thirst I yearned to quench,
Tears countless have my shirt drenched.
A play of the Magician is this world of ours,
My abode lies beyond the stars.
From there I came to this madhouse called the world by the "sane",
Where hate governs the tribe and ignorance is not a bane.
In this realm of strangers till when shall I pass time,
Remaining alive while articulating my anguish in rhyme.
When shall Thee come O Master of divinity untold?
I wait to seek Thy benedictions before the work unfolds.

11

The Divine King Maker

Sing my mind of the saga divine,
Though occurring in space yet transcending time.
This shall be sung by bards of all ages,
All shall receive its bounty in various stages.
The epic of the land of sages,
Where truth is entrapped within mazes.
In the clan of the Yadus Divinity incarnated,
The Supreme Person playing roles as fate dictated.
Providence had to intervene many times,
To restore the rightful to the Pandavas devoid of any
crime.

12

The Universal Paradox

The Universe sings of His glory,
There is a sublime sermon in the cuckoo's story.
Hear Him when the birds chirp,
Or behold Him while little children play in mirth.
Blessed indeed is this planet earth,
Teeming with life even in its dirt.
Man His creation does on a pedestal stand,
For it is up to him to know the Creator in the rainbow's strands.
The Lord pervades the creation and yet stands apart,
In Him all contradictions arise such is His very art.
A paradox He is that none could explain,
How can mere mortals comprehend Him with their puny brain.
I must smile when the thieving mind tries to grasp Him,
It is easier for one to fill a tiny pitcher with the entire ocean up its brim.
Yet through Love myriad saints have received His mercy,
For the One who pervades the Universe is present in you and me.

And out of His merciful nature He appears in every age as Man,
What a miracle of His that Infinite Divinity in three cubits embodied stands.
When expounding on His glories I must confess my mind reels and there is no rest,
So inconceivable He is that at His behest myriad creations are formed as if in utmost jest.

13

Dignity of the Seeker

To conjure a feat that a mere magician can perform,
To construe ideas and phrases all one's own is the norm.
This is my idea of poetry that shall please all times,
Yet to be inspired by another is not a crime.
Just as the fragrance of the rose pervades in stealth,
In like manner spreads the glory of the Spiritual Self.
Some say that there is no witness to defy,
Yet others in sublime verse do the Self glorify.
Reality they say is an eternal void,
Yet by repeating sutras alone ignorance is never destroyed.
The Being within yearns to attain the cessation of all desires,
Yet the torment inflicted upon the mind is akin to a raging fire.
Know for certain that your such a being the likes of which none has seen,
Just like the pearls hidden in the have in secrecy their being.
Our world is like a bubble in the ocean of the vast cosmos,

Of what consequence is breath to metamorphose?
In a second will this dream end,
Whether beautiful or horrific on you it will depend.
By the Grace of the Master all ties must dissolve,
Then the cosmic mystery shall forever be solved.

14

The Riddle of Love

To find solace for a lover's heart,
Is a task as daunting as playing blindfolded a game of dart.
In the passing of each and every moment,
My soul yearns for the Beloved to end this torment.
Lovers of fickle heart abound in plenty,
Their numbers increase with each passing day multiplied by infinity.
Earthly love I have seen enough to decipher,
Self-interest is the major cause while love is at best minor.
Forsaking these ties of the material world I shall behold Thee in trance,
On the tunes composed by the Beloved I will jump and prance.
Not caring for what the world might say,
In your remembrance I will pass each night and day.

15

Deja vu

Whispers from the silent night,
Flashes of the distant past setting the fire of my memory alight.
In myriad forms I have been here before,
A feeling arises within like waves from ashore.
This bond of love from many incarnations burns,
In the firmament of my heart by leaps and turns.
From where I came is a question
Beyond time's limited frame,
Yet I choose to reveal,
All that a worthy heart can feel.
From beyond the realm of name and form,
I descended to the material world where suffering is the norm.
All I might say will just sound like a bunch of words,
For language cannot go further than its domain like the caged birds.
Articulating my identity is a task most daunting,
What seem like sentences are mere shadows haunting.

Contradictions and incoherent statements linger in my brain,
For I have attained a state beyond the reach of the supposedly sane.
With this I put my pen to rest,
My effort to manifest reality in words ends in mere jest.

16

The Mother Divine

You shower Your bounty of Grace O! Mother,
When my coffers can never store more than a feather.
You are the Ocean of Love Divine,
But my vessel is limited by space and time.
Beyond the limited and supremely infinite,
Thy presence confers on me unlimited delight.
I appeal to You O! Empress of the cosmos entire,
Please rescue me from this worldly quagmire.
When the hour comes and my play be done,
Come to Thy child and unite him with the One.

17

To the Ultimate Godhead

Love is the flame which burns my soul,
Attaining Him is the only goal.
Is it so difficult to the beloved behold?
Your presence graces my heart yet the suffering is untold.
The scriptures say Your heart is like butter which melts,
Yet my yearning which burns every moment is not by you felt.
The night seems immense as an ocean,
Time stands still it seems not in motion.
A moment passes as heavy as lead,
This is the reward for choosing You over the world instead.
Tears copious embellish my chest,
Alas my soul can never find rest.
Without You I am devoid of zest,
If this be Your will then it is best.

18

Love's Strife

When will the blessed day arrive?
Then for the gift of love I shall strive.
This pain in separation is true,
But never do my tears a reward accrue.
I am happy in Thy delight,
For one glace I shall struggle with all my might.
Having abandoned this world and the next,
I shall suffer agony while for You its jest.
Punish me or reward me with Thy love,
You are the veritable treasure trove.
So many nights I have spent in vain,
I accept wholeheartedly Your gift of pain.
One day Your silence shall be eloquent,
Then my love shall find a proper vent.
Till then I will repeat Thy name and cry,
If You come I shall be grateful or otherwise die.

19

Eternal Life

In the confluence of the ages,
Ancient wisdom of the myriad sages.
I remember the past as it may have been,
Many the tales that still lie unseen.
This drama of death and birth,
Is not for mourning but for mirth.
You shall know eternal life,
But for that death must be your wife.
The day you know death there will be life,
Filled with splendour devoid of every strife.
This tale of hide and seek,
Is nothing more than a joke for us to keep.
The Beloved beckons at the shore,
Meet life with zest and the challenges it has in store.

20

Dissolution of the Ego

The immensity of life,
The joy hidden in every strife.
Attaining the ultimate absolute,
Beyond the time dark as soot.
Sorrows I renounce,
Depression I do denounce,
Like the royal cat raring to pounce,
Ecstasy pervades every ounce;
Of my being;
The One which is hidden and unseen.
Love sings the symphony divine,
Erasing the distinctions of me and mine.

21

Glimpse of the Reality

Like a child playing in the field,
So do I wander this planet in zeal.
My Being none can ever steal,
I now have the divine elixir for my meal.
The bliss I feel the tongue can never tell,
Yet heresy it shall be to remain silent as well.
So I try to articulate what belongs to the mind,
Words are mere pointers they alone can never the beloved find.
Devoid of incantations and knowledge,
Intentionally I commit a sacrilege.
Yet I shall sing the song Divine,
May its rhythm strike a chord with mankind.

22

Discovery of the Beloved

My acquaintance of eternity,
My Love for posterity.
When I look in Your eyes,
Your smile does mesmerise.
You possess my soul,
I am a part Thou are the whole.
The reason for my existence sole,
Is to attain life's only goal.
Your love I sought birth after birth,
My existence is filled with mirth.
On finding You my love so true,
No harm can fate ever construe.

23

Divine Wine

The yearning which I for the Beloved feel,
Is beyond words and thoughts can never reveal.
It was experienced by the mind,
My soul revelling in the Self divine.
Words I must use to articulate,
To give a glimpse of the ultimate state.
Lost in translation as they say,
When my mind employs language to make it obey.
The language of Love is known to the heart,
Yet we thirst over the elixir that the Beloved has got.
This gift can never be bought,
All the wealth in the world shall fall short.
This is the wine of the mystic divine,
One glance from the Beloved can inebriate you for many lifetimes.

24

Divine Visit

Today the Beloved came to my door,
He had the gift of Love in store.
I asked Him what shall be the prize,
He replied nothing less than your demise.
Fear gripped my soul,
For my realisation was partial and not whole.
He smiled and said,
I was referring to your ego and not the Self.
The Self is all in all call it one or two,
Yet it is attained only by a handful few.
The fool that I am could not dwell,
And lost the opportunity as well.
Yet I shall yearn with a fervour burning,
Indifferent to fate and fortune which keep turning.
My cries shall melt His heart,
Or with my life I shall part.
This saga of life and death is eternal,
Yet I shall love Him with intensity supernal.

25

Beauty of Divinity

My love for You increases with every breath,
And my ecstasy knows no bound while tears are my wreath.
Remove from Your splendorous face the veil,
I must pinch myself to believe all this is real.
Beauty You possess like I have never seen,
Every tear of longing has attained its dream.
To attain Your vision was my goal,
But now that aim You also stole.
As You please my Beloved Divine,
I too have imprisoned You for all time.

26

Spiritual Yearning

All my days pass in vain,
Not attaining Him I grimace in pain.
My copious tears are not enough to gain,
The vision of the One whose love drives me insane.
Till when shall I suffer the pangs of separation,
Am I condemned to eternal damnation?
Though not consigned to the flames of hell,
Yet the way in which I burn none can ever tell.
May my love attain its worthy end,
And a message the Lord may send.
To console my grieving sole,
For His sake I shall endure grief untold.

27

A Myth Called Death

Must myself be forever lost in oblivion,
Such thoughts plague my mind by the million.
What shall be left of me?
When fate passes the ultimate decree.
When death is at my door,
I shall embrace it all the more.
For you are just a messenger of my Beloved,
And I but a passenger.
You are the veil that I must pierce,
Your look is fierce.
I have learnt your secret though you kept it very well,
I shall never cease to be for I am beyond heaven and hell.
The entity that I call I,
Is more expansive than the sky.
Death may consume this body of flesh and bones,
It has never discriminated between paupers and the ones who sit on thrones.
But when you shall knock on my door,
With a smile I will pass on to the other shore.
There in communion with the Beloved of mine,
I shall live forever transcending space and time.

28

Ecstatic Musings

The mind is filled with ecstasy and heavenly delight,
Now that the Beloved is forever in my sight.
Eternal union this of the soul and the Source,
Fie on the opinions of the worldly who consider it a hoax.
No more are the opinions of the world in my mind they are all in vain,
The sight of the Beloved gives me such pleasure that it justifies all the pain.
The yearning of my soul the world knows not
And about the musings of fool I don't care a jot.
In love with the Beloved I will dance and prance,
No hold of the world can fetter the feet of lovers engrossed in divine trance.

29

A Dialogue with the Beloved

Endless nights of longing and yearning untold,
I pass without sleep for once the Beloved to behold.
When this union delightful shall take place,
I shall behold Thy peerless Face.
Of beauty infinite,
Ever enhancing the lover's delight.
Bliss eternal shall forever be mine,
When I shall His eternal abode find.
Knock I did once upon His door,
Pat came the reply "Come back when thee shall be no more.
When that I of yours ceases and thee transcend me and mine,
Then look into thy heart and there you shall Me find."

30

The Master

A noble patriarch walking down the lane,
His silent eyes eloquently speak a language that none may disdain.
In that glance ascends eternity itself,
I haven't seen you before yet we have certainly met.
Thy gaze tremendous informs me that I might not know you yet I belong to thee.
The illusion ephemeral in which I live will one day come to an end,
Before that fateful moment arrives it is better to my ways mend.
Vanished have the trees, the buildings and everything from the scene,
Yet I sense thy presence divine comforting amidst the dream.
My time as such has not yet come as myriad wait the works to be done,
Yet I know that when you shall beckon to renounce every vestige and be forever One;
I shall not be found wanting and heeding thy call to lose everything is trivial in return of gaining All.

31

Divine Ennui

Many the nights you have spent chasing pleasures
mundane,
Once spend a night sleepless for the Beloved to attain.
The vision beatific will then be revealed to your inner eye,
Till then the words of deep longing let your soul satisfy.
Though I write in the form of verse and let words speak
my pain,
Yet the language of the heart knows none except the
Beloved whose favour I may gain.
To articulate in the words of the world the anguish of my
soul,
Is a task akin to filling a tiny pitcher of water with a vast
ocean untold .
Yet I try to express my urge in words ignoring the
limitations of language infinite,
That some consolation may reach my grief stricken soul
and I might gain some respite.

32

The Universal Delusion

Like the fragrance in the navel of the musk deer,
We seek Thee afar when you are forever near.
I have wandered the wild world in search of Thine,
Yet Thy presence eternal I could never find.
I saw you there when I looked at my own soul,
To seek Thee is a journey long and not some trivial goal.
With open eyes I did the globe search,
But when I looked inside I discovered endless mirth.
A joy unconditioned, uncaused transcending space and time,
Is a bounty bestowed upon the fortunate few by the treasurer Divine.
I forever do in this bliss revel,
Soaked in ecstasy beyond heaven and hell.

33

Ephemeral Existence

Divine love beckons me to act,
To do everything after signing the Pact;
With the Beloved who can tell,
When my ego bloats and begins to swell.
He shows me I was nothing and All was He.
Without Him no creation could ever be.
Hence he veils His real face,
Under Maya's influence we grimace.
If I had only known that this play unreal,
The agony that scorched my heart would have seemed trivial.
Alas how ignorant I have been?
Searched without all along but never glanced within.
You are the Truth eternal and sublime,
What I called 'I' was just a myth in time.

34

Conquest of the Beloved

I will capture You with my love,
Engage You like a beautiful dove.
The symbol of beauty and peace,
Ever so young and eternally sweet.
The feather of Love you always bore,
Of Ecstasy utmost You are the Source.
In symbols I embellish You,
Your's is the only Love that is true.
One with closed eyes can never see the day,
Ignorance is the barrier much to the seeker's dismay.
Yet I shall strive and stop never,
Stealing You from the existence forever.

35

Divine Anxiety

Love is its own reward some say,
But what kind of Love can ignorance slay?
The end might justify the means,
I shall endeavour forever so as to glimpse the Scene;
Of heavenly delight.
The earth bound senses are obsolete,
This saga of celebration it can never keep.
What does it matter if I lose my identity?
To revel in the Bliss of the Beloved for all eternity.

36

Priceless Devotion

Love of the flesh can be bought,
Thus it is most sought.
I do not condemn the senses for they point towards the stars,
Yet they cannot reach even as far as Mars.
Devotion alone is the true rocket,
Which can knock out the sockets;
Of a life immersed in the senses,
Love true is beyond all the tenses.
Love is not an emotion but the life force of the entire Creation,
The one who attains this gift is free from damnation.
When love is of the body we term it as lust,
When we yearn for water they term it as thirst.
When it exists between two souls we call it corporeal attraction,
While when it exists for all we term it a token from Above.

37

The Wordly Wizard

My mind begins to ponder,
And self begins to wonder.
What have I attained or committed a blunder,
The ties of the world begin to cut asunder.
By the sword of wisdom and knowledge,
Of learning beyond any school or college.
Here the curriculum is Divine inebriation,
To connect to the Source beyond all creation.
The sages and prophets of yore,
Here they settle their ultimate score.
The job that one gets on graduation,
Is of unbounded Love towards the entire Creation.
Mere information collected in the brain,
That remains for a duration and then fades in vain.
Is not Education as I define,
Let character building and inner strength be inculcated
in this precious time.

38

Literary Might

My words are the weapons I yield,
To defeat ignorance and form the ultimate shield.
Words can open diverse vistas and set new paradigms,
I intend to demolish the limited conceptions of mankind.
The greatest respect I have for the traditions of the world,
But their limitations I strive to eliminate from the bud.
Organised religion does not touch my soul,
Transcendence should be your only goal.
Wealth is enough to necessary comforts buy,
Beyond that its paper neither useful to you or I.
In this world of materialistic longings I cannot explain,
The pain that people go through striving for only material gain.
I do not intend to preach nor do I care to cheat,
With our needs satisfied money is reduced to worthless sheets.
Yet the disparity of wealth screams in my face,
A statistic of unequal distribution the ultimate disgrace.

39

The Deadly Boon

Take me by the hand my Lord,
When time unleashes its fatal sword.
May I not be wanting in faith of Thee,
As death knocks on my door and summons me.
Leaving this mortal coil behind,
I will fly beyond the realm of time.
As the final breath does depart,
My soul shall sever the knot of bondage apart.
With You as my guide and Love eternal,
I will attain Thy abode of bliss supernal.

40

Religion of Love

My Beloved is the source of all love,
He dwells in each heart and yet up above.
To fear him is a heresy most condemned,
In the religion of Love where He is the best friend.
Closer than the closest yet He appears afar,
To attain Him, Love alone is the polestar.
Fear your deeds and not the Divine,
He is the most munificent benefactor of all mankind.
When man tries to know His ways I must smile,
It is like making a paper boat and attempting to cross the river Nile.
To the lips that quiver out of fear is denied the wine of the divine,
Embellish instead your eyes with tear or longing and soon you shall Him find.

41

Descent of Divinity

When the Divine descends in human form,
He transcends all bonds and breaks every norm.
The same can be said of the ordinary soul,
Yet it embodies in part the Divinity of an Incarnation untold.
The Power that empowers them is the same,D
Yet the degree of manifestation is different and will shall ever remain.
I speak not from the mantle of a prophet grown old,
But from wisdom immense which from the Soul unfolds.
To understand the Divinity encaged in corporeal embellishment,
Is a task so arduous that it transcends all comment.
Fools lost in the worldly grammar,
When trying to recognise the Supreme must cough and stammer.
They never could decipher their own reality,
Yet they deride and attempt to understand the Supreme verity.
The task is as feasible to your tiny brain,
As To expect sermons of wisdom from the insane.

42

The Divine Cowherd

O Beloved of oceanic hue,
The One whose lies seem to be true.
You sport in every epoch as a human being,
Yet infinite forms of Thine still remain unseen
Although You are the embodiment of Godhead supreme,
Yet the love of devotees drags You from Thy realm of dreams.
The affection of your votaries draws You to this world of impermanence,
Such love for Thy servants You have that it cannot be expressed in a sentence.
Yet I try to do what can never be done to articulate the mystic of Love,
Which propounds the doctrine that You live in my Heart and not up above.
The sacrifice that You make in descending to this world of death,
Is the greatest gift that Thy lovers can ever get.
Your advent makes the clarion call,
Of love divine to one and all.

Without Thy Love my longing will drown me in an ocean of tears,
When shall I behold Thy face the vanquisher of all fears?
Counting each breath I live to prepare myself for union with Thee,
Will the longing of my heart ever be accepted as a valid plea?
The future I have surrendered at Thy feet,
Yet if my yearning shall remain incomplete.
I will wait for aeons and incarnations infinite,
When finally we will play the flute together with delight.

43

The Saga of Vanity

Days keep passing and memories fade,
Relentless time marches on with its blade.
Many have fallen and countless more will drown,
In the tide of time that engulfs all around.
What shall remain of this is a wonder,
When the axe falls upon our neck with a blunder.
In this instant of Cosmic Time I will revise,
For what purpose was this gift of life?
The Beloved was ever etched in my heart and soul,
To meet Him was my life's ultimate goal.
Within and without I searched all around,
Yet no trace of His could be found.
The body has dropped like a leaf abandoned by the tree,
Now there remains no distinction between Him and me.
The pot of clay has been broken to find,
The separation existed only in the mind.
Adorned with the Bliss of the Beloved Supreme,
I ceases to exist as if it were only a dream.
Awakened have I from the pretentions of slumber,

Now I myself am the Beloved nothing remains to wonder.
In Words to convey my rapture is a futile exercise,
Yet language being the only tool at my disposal I choose to strive.
To convey in words that which only silence could tell,
As feasible a task as making Heaven of Hell.
With this I put an end to the chatter in my mind,
I will retire to the solitary sanctuary of the Heart so as to Him find.

44

The Night of Delight

The world is immersed in deep slumber,
But to the Yogi the night is filled with wonder.
On so many nights you have remained asleep,
But with my Beloved I shall soon speak.
The sounds of quiet is not a mere figure of speech,
But to the lovers is the dialect in which spirits preach.
From Heart to heart and Soul to soul,
Is the music which in utter silence unfolds.
Volumes can be written about a single sentence,
Wisdom exudes knowledge like a choicest fragrance.
In the language of the Heart I converse with my Love,
Words remain unspoken yet the silence is like a lovely dove.
Pristine in its beauty and untouched by stains,
Only a peacock can match its beauty during the rains.
Parallels I draw from the kingdom of birds,
For their prattle though spoken cannot be heard.
No heed a human being pays to their distant calls,
They too converse like Masters in silence so as to ignorance maul.

These creatures live in touch with Mother Nature,
This fact alleviates their stature.
In the eyes of arrogant humanity,
Which is driving with each passing day unto insanity.
Countless ages have passed chasing gifts ephemeral,
For once I desire the joy of bliss supernal.
From now I shall pray in the silence of the night,
To the Knave who steals hearts and fills them with eternal delight.

45

Ruthless Violence and Musings in Silence

The footsteps of spring arrive in silence,
Nature has been exploited by humanity's violence.
I perceive the Divine in each and every leaf,
The one who robs Nature is a despicable thief.
There is enough for mankind's need,
But none can satisfy immense greed.
Hoarding wealth without any qualm,
Today has been established as the norm.
O! Man you must realize to whom does this belong,
Transitory are your treasures renounce some and be strong.
I sing as a bard a hymn to the Highest Divinity,
Shower Thy Grace on the ignorant existent in plenty.

46

Counsel to the Mind

Must you seek always without,
And be plagued with all the doubts.
Why must you roam around like a fool?
Setting your eyes in filth you constantly drool.
You are the cause of bondage and yet also the greatest tool,
To emancipate from the world and end the eternal duel.
Between the soul and matter,
As well as the mind and its constant chatter.
The one who can still consciousness at his behest,
Has passed the penultimate test.
From this 'school' called life,
And now reigns supreme over each and every strife.

47

A Celebration Called Life

Each day now I celebrate,
Every passing moment is great.
Even anguish in Love is pleasure,
For then do the sentiments increase beyond measure.
Distance they say makes the heart go fonder,
But I add it also makes us stronger.
The gift of Love none can ever rob,
It inebriates you whether you are alone or in a mob.
There is no benediction like Love,
And there never can be an addiction like Love.

48

The Apparent Truth

Each day passes like a second in time,
Fleeting is my verse in rhyme.
By inquiry of the intellect I certainly do not find,
The walls within my psyche of the past left behind.
The past is history as they say,
The present alone is the 'truth' their counsels convey.
The future is a mystery which none could solve,
Yet I hope my trespasses are absolved.
Every moment I have spent in sin not as the books might tell,
Though appearing to be in Heaven I have circumscribed the depths of Hell.
These realms of the afterlife could very well be true,
Yet these are all pervasive states of consciousness that our mind drew.

49

Love's Reward

Forgetting all difficulties my soul does rejoice,
I play with the Beloved day and night.
He is with me forever whose company I had dreamt,
Eternal is His charm as He shines in my heart's firmament.
Both within and without is He,
There is not a place where He cannot be.
Without His presence none can possibly exist,
To think otherwise is a heresy which I desist.
His manifestation varies in the myriad creation,
The realization of Truth is the cause of the greatest celebration.
That is the state to which a seeker can possibly evolve,
And the solution to the Ultimate Riddle that none could ever solve.

50

A Saga Called Life

This saga spanning eternity,
Is the Universal Dream reaching infinity.
One fine day we will get up and wonder,
And laugh at this blunder.
It all was a play of many births,
There was a lot of pain yet some mirth.
What we struggled to attain,
Shed tears of joy and also of pain.
Now only the memories remain,
Conscience is free from all stain.
Like adepts at the game of life,
We prepare for each and every strife.
Having learnt our lessons we shall forever be free,
Life is the only Truth while death the greatest myth to ever be.

51

The Mother Divine

Though anguish assaulted me day and night,
Yet I withstood its boundless might.
For my Mother was never out of sight,
Who comforted me and brought me to the abyss of delight.
In Her I attained the fulfilment of all my dreams,
I saw Her as I see the world but in a manner even more serene.
She fondled me in Her lap and played hide and seek,
Here I was sought by One whose presence even the gods could not keep.
Myriad creations move with Her mere brow,
Can life possibly a greater boon bestow?

52

The Universal Delusion

Time trickles by,
Ages it does defy.
What fraction is 'life'?
In the scheme of the cosmos our very own strife.
An exercise in vanity of the mind,
Deluded by appearances of every kind.
Yet not knowing the Essence behind,
Of Love being the ruler of space and time.
Many shadows lurk in the dark of the night,
Phantoms of our creation stare at us in all their might.
Our own delusion haunts through myriad lifetimes,
None is responsible for our conditioning of space and
time.

53

The Quest for Freedom

A day shall arrive when people may tell this unworthy scribe,
To speak less in altruisms and the heavenly dimensions less describe.
Though I am unworthy yet I for certain know,
Spirituality is not a mere block that you can pass along or throw.
Language does not do justice to the trials and agony in which I have burned,
Just in order to experience a second of stillness how my soul has yearned.
Putting my life on the line and suffering the void in my own mind,
Battling anxieties and anguish I never stood behind.
Instead I faced these problems and looked them in the eye,
They might be strong but I am much stronger inside.

54

The Circus of the Mind

Another beautiful day in my life,
As I discover that the mind is the source of all strife,
The mind is the one that binds yet it liberates,
Though the goal is still distant yet it celebrates.
Do not ever give in to the vagaries of the mind,
It will destroy your sanity and leave you behind.
On the path of blessedness it is a cheat I must say,
Only a hero can subdue it and make it obey.
Instead of reading books observe your own mind,
How it forms impressions and habits labelling them as vile or divine.

55

On Poetry

Words appear from the void and flow,
What is this gift which seems to grow.
Never for once did I desire poetic creation,
Unasked came this skill of literary innovation.
Perhaps there is a task which destiny deemed fit,
There might be an ulterior reason for this Divine Gift.
What that may be I am without a clue,
Perhaps Love knows its own course which destiny construes.
Whenever I reflect and contemplate,
Words my mind conjures and fill the empty slate.
As the fisherman throws a bait,
I weave another rhyme and my mind gyrates.

56

Fatal Love

To Love is to die,
Here I speak of the ego and not 'I'.
The ones who Love none can ever kill,
Yet doubts assail me and my mind I am unable to still.
Mortals like us may come and go,
But 'Love' transcends space and time this for certain I know.
I might not remain in this mortal coil for eternity,
Yet my identity shall live within the Beloved for all posterity.
In losing 'me' I shall forever gain 'you',
Blessed are the kind hearted who receive this gift reserved for a fortunate few.

57

Eternal Sojourn of the Mind

Today I shall tell you of the Immense Glory,
Of my Beloved but who can narrate His story?
Even if I sing for a million lifetimes,
Like a prisoner articulating Love in time.
We can always demark and define,
What is tangible and not yours or mine.
But His Love belongs to the world,
And so the banner of His ship is unfurled.
The world seeks happiness and joy,
As men we seek pleasure while in childhood we pursued toys.
The happiness we received was transient yet there,
From where did it come and why did it leave us in despair?
The Love and Bliss you sought for aeons of lifetimes,
Was rooted in ignorance yet never a crime.
Let those failures be left behind,
Just as diamonds receive blows let that be a metaphor for your mind.

58

The Jewel Within

When I look within,
I perceive the Beloved Divine.
Each moment of my life is yours; the rest a delusion of the mind,
May I receive Your Divine Embrace and sorrows be left behind.
With every breath may I cherish Your Name,
You are the possessor of eternal fame.
Yet a few seek You to obtain only Your Grace,
While others wish to behold Thy Peerless Face.
The One who manifested myriad galaxies by a mere smile,
To seek You I have travelled and covered innumerable miles.
I was awake yet dreaming a dream,
Now I am fully awake in the Self Supreme.

59

A Utopian Fantasy

Where there shall be no norms,
No dichotomy between right and wrong.
There I shall wait for You,
Far beyond fate's construe.
A land where dwells only Truth beyond reason,
Where bliss is the only festival of each season.
I do not lie when such a destination is near,
Where there is no possibility of fear.
Such a land I intend to attain in this lifetime,
Breaking the shackles of the mind.
There I shall find the One whom I sought forever,
Living in His abode with ever renewed fervour.
For I have attained a state beyond the reach of the supposedly sane.
With this I put my pen to rest,
My effort to manifest reality in words ends in mere jest.

60

Eternity of Life

Whispers from the silent night,
Flashes of the distant past setting the fire of my memory alight.
In myriad forms I have been here before,
A feeling arises within like waves from ashore.
This bond of love from many incarnations burns,
In the firmament of my heart by leaps and turns.
From where I came is a question
beyond time's limited frame,
Yet I choose to reveal,
All that a worthy heart can feel.
From beyond the realm of name and form,
I descended to the material world where suffering is the norm.
All I might say will just sound like a bunch of words,
For language can not go further than its domain like the caged birds.
Articulating my identity is a task most daunting,
What seem like sentences are mere shadows haunting.
Contradictions and incoherent statements linger in my brain,

61

Cosmic Worship

Revelling in the silent night,
In raptures is my life, a mart of delight.
The firmament of the stars I employ for His adoration,
Each and every galaxy along with all the particles of His creation.
Such an altar may I prepare,
To do justice to the Divinity who is ever now and here.
Many nights I have spent weeping,
Though awake yet pretending to be sleeping.
For the Beloved I could have waited aeons,
This world it seems is a blend of His crayons.
Yet my Sweetheart complied for the union of the soul,
Where the 'I' is lost and yet the soul experiences bliss untold.

62

The Beatific Vision

Without Love you can never attain,
Obtaining His vision relinquished is all pain.
What is the difference that shall remain?,
When we behold the One devoid of any stain.
He has endowed the land with myriad grains,
He is the Supreme Giver but loved in truth by only the 'insane'.
How distinct are His devotees who for His service renounce hearth and home,
Instead they worship Him in the temple of their hearts using the mantra Om .
Though Invincible He can be conquered by Love,
For His devotees He is the Ultimate Treasure Trove.

63

Unspeakable Truth

Words and more words are what we throw around,
Their interpretations are as different as their distinct sounds.
Yet they are all we have to reveal,
The esoteric truth which at best one can only feel.
From the language of the world I do steal,
Its treasures which are ephemeral yet seem real.
That the world is a mere illusion I do not stake a claim,
Yet I do not consider 'Truth' that which is subject to change.

64

Anguish of the Soul

These days of pain I shall remember till eternity,
Unheard is such pain in the medical fraternity.
There is no fire yet I burn,
Healthy is my body yet painful each and every turn.
Of sorrow are my tears,
That leave me with joy and eradicate all fears.
These are the gifts of Love whose beauty only the most fortunate can see,
Blessed am I beyond imagination having received Fate's decree.
The times of burning I leave behind,
Now I can revel at last in bliss divine.
Farewell to the ego of me and mine,
A solution to the eternal riddle I did find.

65

The Spiritual Master

The Master is my sole treasure,
To have Him I am blessed beyond measure.
The greatest creation of God,
My companion on solitary ways I trod.
To express even a tinge of His greatness I am unworthy,
Yet my faith is fragile and not sturdy.
He gave me the Elixir of Divine Love from His store,
Since then I am inebriated longing for more.
With a single glance He can alter destiny and rewrite fate,
For He has attained the most sublime State.

66

The Existential Crisis

Perhaps I was born to ruin my destiny,
Searching for Him who alone could bless me.
Yet this search has proved to be a failure,
My very self-burns under the myriad layers.
Of tears, blood and sweat I smell,
Searching for You but I am in Hell.
Of doubt, anguish and defeat,
Yet my desired end I have failed to meet.
My identity is a burden which I am yet to discover,
Yet bereaved under its weight I continuously suffer.
Depression is an under estimate of my condition,
It seems I have been doomed to perdition.

67

Manacles of the Mind

The chimeras that plague the mind,
Are our own creations and not divine.
When one may glimpse the Self eternal,
I shall attain joy supernal.
Such bliss as none could possibly feel,
This state is such that even time cannot steal.
In a single moment everything was revealed,
Even in ignorance I possessed the indestructible shield;
Granted by the Mother Divine,
She is the Ultimate Teacher as she is eternity transcending time.
How in words can I describe Her glory?
Like the boundless ocean is Her story.

68

Immaculate Love

The religion of love does not require the sword,
May you dwell in the immaculate abode.
Where there are no boundaries to divide,
And all one has to do is confide.
In the Architect of the Divine Plan,
Love which unites man and man.
Let them usher an age of affection and laughter,
The one who knows how to live both here and hereafter.
Compassion is the key while to serve is my plea,
One must face adversaries and never try to flee.
This is the attitude which imparts victory,
To serve is to worship you may consider our history.

69

Transformation of the Soul

Sing of my Love to the blue sky,
Forget these boundaries and attain perennial joy.
Today I have vanquished the formidable 'I',
Once again I have become a little child.
Beautiful hearts they have as they dwell in constant wonder,
No excuses but only smiles cover up their every blunder.
The children they say are in the likeness of God I do remember,
They are the inheritors of Heaven and of Bliss perpetual vendors.
Christ I am told said that the Divine Vision only the pure in heart can see,
Not mine neither yours this perhaps is Providence's Ultimate Decree.

70

Divine Anguish

On this day what I can desire?
My being, my very soul is on fire.
The thirst I yearned to quench,
Tears countless have my shirt drenched.
A play of the Magician is this world of ours,
My abode lies beyond the stars.
From there I came to this madhouse called the world by the "sane",
Where hate governs the tribe and ignorance is not a bane.
In this realm of strangers till when shall I pass time,
Remaining alive while articulating my anguish in rhyme.
When shall Thee come O Master of divinity untold?
I wait to seek Thy benedictions before the work unfolds.

71

Love's Paradox

My heart is no longer in my control,
It seems my mind has left for a stroll.
To attain the Pristine Love I strive day and night,
My soul feels numb as if bombarded by a dynamite.
Yet it is not all pain that I suffer,
But the riddle I intend to decipher.
Silent screams and lucid dreams,
It seems as if I am consigned to an endless stream.
Though I struggle with all my might,
Yet I can not explain this painful delight.
Love of the corporeal can be easily expressed,
But what to say of love that brings sweet stress.

72

Advise to the Mind

Oh my mind why do you roam in expectations from humankind,
The day shall come when you shall leave all of it behind.
Making strangers your dear most friends,
Not thinking about your penultimate end.
Till when shall you delude me with this lie,
Taking appearances for the Truth you falsely testify.
Return to the abode from which you did descend,
Opening a market of bliss you received only suffering in the end.
The time shall come when you shall go,
And then only a stranger will row;
Your boat across this ocean of ignorance,
That stranger is the Beloved untouched by all the nescience.

73

A Prayer to the Mother

O Mother do visit my house,
Privileged is Shiva to have You as His spouse.
Thought the epitome of sinners I might be,
Yet Your name will save me from Fate's decree.
To attain You one must perform austerities so the scriptures speak,
But only Love can draw You to the holy and the meek.
Without learning or special qualification was I,
Yet Thy grace made me all obstacles defy.
This is the magic of our Love and affection I must say,
Indeed the internal demons You have forever slayed.
A fool like me attained the ultimate goal of life,
To attain You is simple while the world plagued with strife.

74

Love for Writing

Now I see the path that calls,
A life which shall boredom maul.
Making such an occupation as my own vocation,
Is a dream which is even better than vacation .
As the trains leave the myriad stations,
My false self is now in the stage of cremation.
Tomorrow shall come with good tidings,
When all my time I shall devote to writing.
This is the unearthly grace of the Lord with the mace,
Who at times appears with a magnificently beautiful face.
Your remembrance and contemplation is my only goal,
From Your own abode by my Love You forever I stole.
And enshrined You within my heart,
From now on Your my prisoner as Thee I have caught.

75

Inexplicable Bliss

Now each moment is ecstatic immersed in perennial delight,
My soul sings of the love it has for the One with boundless might.
My days whirl like the Sufis of yore,
While nights are with the Beloved who of transcendental bliss is the store.
Finally my love bears fruit with the golden dawn,
The tears and lamentations that adorned my person are now forlorn.
May my life be a prayer unto Thee,
What else can I offer having forgotten in love even 'me'?

76

Grace of the Master

Many a times did I cry my heart out,
When the Beloved did not arrive leaving me perplexed with doubts.
Institutions never gave me solace,
My questions shattered superstitions with a mace.
But then when the day arrived,
My life was transformed and I for perfection strived.
By just a look He altered the course of my life,
Though doubts at certain junctions did arise yet I was without any strife.
The magic glance you can call it as you may,
The soul since that incident strived for perfection and was never in disarray.

77

God's Ungodly World

In this world where materialism is rampant and so is pain,
Where countless die an untimely death and invite Fate's disdain.
Love external relishes the senses of touch, smell and sight,
Begins beautifully but ends in terrible fights.
There must be a road on course which must delight,
Each and every traveller in this world struggling with might.
To defeat the foes external one might strive,
But more difficult is to conquer the demon called 'I'.
This ego a product of the misidentification of the mind,
Is the worst disease embedded in the psyche we find.
This is not a game for the week,
Only Heroes of valour extraordinary can seek;
The treasure that lies beyond time,
Gaining access to that which transcends 'me' and 'mine'.

78

Karma-The Ultimate Retribution

Let the strings of the lute sing,
Prophecies from the I Ching.
All are curious as to what Fate has in store,
Why do some receive less and others more?
This is the question none can ever tell,
Yet we believe in Heaven and ignore Hell.
Perhaps Hell is for the ones who never knew,
Our actions determine Destiny and they stick to us like glue.
Aeons might pass yet one must reap,
The actions of ignorance and climb the mountain most steep.
Divinities whose actions are inscrutable and diverse,
Have to suffer the consequences of their deeds for better or worse.
This is the Almighty Law of Karma,
Without it there can never be True Dharma.

79

Love: The Ultimate Obligation

May I breathe my last singing Thy Name,
Thou art the only entity with Eternal Fame.
Hollow are the values of this world we seek,
This is the secret which the seers keep.
We too know the end in a partial sense,
Yet we are not transformed and sell our conscience for a few cents.
In the Cosmic Plan what is our life span?
A mere fraction of a second my dear man.
Never waste this gem of life,
Obliterate from your heart every strife.
Revel always in love and delight,
Serve with your hands and love with all thy might.

80

Linguistic Frailties

The obligation of love,
Is the essence of Divinity we seek up above.
My words I decorate in rhyme,
Seeking them to express what language can never define.
Yet they are my only tool,
To express my knowledge yet acknowledging I am a fool.
For who can describe the sentiments of the mind,
A new language must be invented yet pessimism at every step I find.
So as I speak I shall reflect,
Secrets are myriad yet the key is too far kept.

81

Divine Bondage

Till when shall my heart beat?
Till when shall my soul weep?
The appearance of Love till when shall He keep?
Why does He keep delaying the instant we shall meet?
You must have the heart of a Butcher to deny,
For my heart is mine and not yours to occupy.
Since the day You enchanted me,
All I have known is Thee.
Yet Heartless is Your Decree,
Either remove my anguish or set me from the shackles free.

82

The Wedding Supernal

Sometimes I feel like a cloud of delight,
Yet I am ashamed beyond all might.
I chose You as the Sole Love of my life,
Vacillate my fortunes between Love and strife.
Yet the moments I spend with Thee are opulent beyond degree,
This is the panacea of my life otherwise filled with misery.
You are the Life of my soul,
Always by my side yet difficult to behold.
Perhaps a day will come when You will be mine soon,
As my soul shall be the bride and You its Eternal Groom.

83

Pain of Indifference

Songs I write yearning and burning with torment intense,
When will this pain desert me and liberate me from its clutches immense.
Never did I know the extent of Divine Love,
It does delight but when it pains you feel above the burning stove.
To tell the riddle of my mind is a task that I must leave behind,
For it is beyond sanity and rationality transcending even the mind.
Wretched is my life as I have not attained the mission of my life,
Which was to obtain a glance of the Face that removes all strife.
It is always easier said than done,
But what hope lies for the emancipation of the most wretched one?
I might be despicable in all that I have done,
Yet Thou art the only hope if I ever had one.

84

Religion of Love not Bondage

When my eyes close for eternity,
On opening them I shall gain You for posterity.
You I have attained by my heart felt tears and not austerity,
The kriyas of the Yogis I do not know,
Yet Love from my heart always flows.
Without esoteric mantras and incantations,
I woo the Creator of all creations.
Without scriptural study and being a fool of the first order,
What can I make of the sacred texts, so why bother?
Yet You have to arrive in front of Thy poor child,
I am not frightened though the pundits describe You as wild.
They have not tasted the manna from Thy Hands,
Losing their ways in the scriptures they do not know for Whom they stand.

85

Poetry as Worship

I seek forever the creator of my soul,
To attain whose feet is my penultimate goal.
Some sing hymns while the other read scriptures,
So as to make the perfect combination by using these mixtures,
I am devoid of any talent or intellectual brilliance,
Yet words in my mind keep up the fight with resilience.
My writings are the creations of my mind,
Vouching to worship the Supreme Divine.
This is my way to pray and contemplate,
I now keep the mind blank as a slate.
On contemplation words form and make a rhyme,
I plead with the Almighty to absolve all my crimes.
This is my worship and the religion I pursue,
Each has His own way and I have one too.

86

Benedictions of Love

Blessings are myriad like stars,
They might seem distant yet forever they are ours.
Curses are few in numbers yet we commit the age old blunder,
Allotting undue importance to their existence and we wonder;
How come there is no joy in the tale of life?
Why are its pages marred with only strife?
Happiness is pretty much your own creation,
It might seem external yet it is an inner realisation.
Your thoughts are your sole creation,
On them depends your ultimate destination.
Think and contemplate on the Divine,
Whose very legacy is ever new joy transcending time.
Being concise I end this rhyme and this much I will say,
Let the bodies decay for dust they are but never be in dismay.

87

The Treasure Beyond Measure

I have exhausted the ideas from my repertoire yet I shall write,
Only after completing my verses shall I gain respite.
Even if that means to be up all night,
For I write to please the One with Limitless Might.
I might lack words and the way to express,
But the Lord is Omniscient none can He be transgressed.
He shall gift me with a rhyme,
To glorify not Himself but to make me a mortal beyond time.
I have committed many crimes and unworthy I consider myself to be,
Yet He chose me out of His very own limitless mercy.
By His grace the blind gain sight and the lame climb hills,
Only by His Benediction does the yogi his mind stills.

88

Spiritual Evolution

The Supreme Love I desire of You,
Attaining which one is beyond Fate's construe.
When shall a wretch like me attain His Love,
Though I am despicable yet You are the Treasure Trove.
I lack the senses to perceive Thy Divine Glory,
Till I am so gifted I shall only read Your stories.
But without You I can never be,
I think less of myself but more of Thee.
You are the One behind the scenes,
The One who fulfilled all my dreams.
You made me learn many lessons of life,
Happy I was but not yet beyond strife.
The evolution goes for myriad lifetimes,
A soul needs to be tested before reaching the ultimate
paradigm.

89

Life is a dream

My heart is joyous while my Being is exhilarated,
Is this the state to which I have been fated?
Now the sufferings of the past,
Seem like little dreams that left me aghast.
They were not real so to say,
And illusory are the sentiments which seem to hold sway;
Over our life which was forever immersed in strife.
Now that I witnessed the grand spectacle I know,
Life is a dream and so is its every woe.

90

Creation of Love

I celebrate the birth of Divinity,
Not in external forms but merely in me.
This is a day of a new dawn,
The grief and negativity is all gone.
An era commences filled by Love,
Gone is the bitterness I swear by Jove.
Let the musical instruments resound,
The ecstasy of Love knowing no bounds.
In the ears the Divine Music rings,
Near the head the angles sing.
Now I am immersed in ecstatic delight,
No longer exists the dichotomy between wrong and right.
This creation is an act of celebration,
The outpouring of Love and of the Absolute's
deliberation.

91

A Relic Called Love

In the ancient stories of yore,
Love was the ultimate store.
Personification of Divinity,
Stretching to infinity.
Love was not human but Divine,
It is difficult to put in words of rhyme.
Yet without further ado,
I glorify the One who is Ancient yet Ever New.
That is my Beloved the home of paradox,
To write about Him I am at a loss.
Not merely of language do I suffer deficit,
How can one describe the object of many myths?
Stories there are many to tell,
But Truth remains silent as well.

92

Ephemeral Pleasures

I seek a companionship without its physical trappings,
Now I conceive of sensual pleasures as bird droppings.
A body made of dust which shall someday kiss the earth,
Though our house is burning each second we are engrossed in mirth.
Heedless of the tragedy belonging to each mortal,
Death consists of vast portals.
Which can be accessed in trance not solely in a dream,
You are not the body but the Self Supreme.
Many identities you have assumed and all of them were ephemeral,
What good is this viscous circle of Heaven and Hell?
This world burning with the flames of desire,
Equally contaminated with Fate's ire.
Wars are fought and territories sought for occupation,
Causing a threat so deadly that it could lead to human extinction.
In the guise of advancement we are promoting death and disease,
As a need for nurturing and celebrating the ego which will grow like a monster till humankind's very existence cease.

93

Puny Yet Grand

In conversation with Nature,
I reflect on our puny stature.
Galaxies die and many appear,
In like fashion we are born and disappear.
Not anymore than an ephemeral fashion trend,
Our bodies shall be reduced to ashes notwithstanding the tears of your best friend.
The next time if you choose to come again,
Let not your emotions drive you insane.
For in this madhouse of the world none can claim,
Joy everlasting transcending all pain.

94

Cosmic Mother

How can I comprehend Your ways my Mother,
My intellect is finite and in a spot of bother.
You command the Universe and hold it in Your sway,
I am but a minute worm caught in the labyrinth of Thy way.
I depend on You for every chore of mine,
By Thy Grace everything with me is divine.
Thy love is so sacred and pristine,
I have felt it in the waking state as well as in dream.
My Love for You increases every hour,
Love alone can bind You such is its power.
May my heart ever sing of Thy love,
The panacea for all ills and it is also a treasure trove.

95

Psychomachia

I have endlessly yearned,
My soul which has constantly burned.
Now the ego has been turned,
To ashes fit for the urn.
At last I am united with the Lord of my Soul,
And achieved my life's only goal.
In ecstatic delight now I do sing,
In the glory of the King of kings.
Love has filled each pore of my skin,
Finally the battle of the soul I did win.

96

The Union with the Unknowable

It is bound to happen in my life,
When I will behold the vanquisher of all strife.
Infinite would be my delight,
When Time bows to immeasurable might.
The Lovers have their own creed,
But the distinctions of society they never heed.
Love is the sole object they require,
And the status of madness they immediately acquire.
False are these accusations of insanity,
They apply instead to the participants exercising vanity.
Where death is certain and life only a play,
The director is Providence and our task to obey.

97

Universal Mother of Endless Love

A debt that I can't repay,
Of love eternal here to stay.
The Divine who comes as mother,
A reflection of affection on a feather.
A conduit of love supramental,
Yet appearing as human with no mantle.
No pretensions of the outer garb,
Yet of love never debarred.
I thank you for being the polestar,
Being distant yet never afar.
Contradictions arrive when I articulate in words,
Thy dovelike purity incomparable with another bird.

98

Beads of Divinity

The rosary of Love is not restricted to the beads you repeat,

To pray is to wear the rosary of breath and never miss a single beat;

Of your heart and forget all else,

Wisdom is nothing unless it leads to the knowledge of the Self.

The Self for one is no antagonistic to the Divine Lord,

They appear two as the sword and its scabbard.

Yet in essence they are identical,

Without one the other would be a mere construct mental.

To realise God is possible if you care,

No good shall ever be achieved by a mere stare (Tratak).

These activities might give you a disciplined mind,

But to attain Him these are mere pretences which cause further grind.

First attain Love by contemplation which shall soften your heart,

Then yearn for His vision and cry thinking Him to be apart.

Slowly tears of Love will be showered by your eyes,
And that day is not far when the you will realise;
Sadhana is its own prize,
And God vision is the surmise.

Tratak: A form of focusing your gaze on a stationary object for varied duration of times ranging from a single minute to some hours. It is believed that such a practice leads to stillness of the mind and consequently enhances concentration useful not only in worldly endeavours but in meditation too.

Sadhana: It simply means to perfect something. In this context it is considered to be a spiritual practice based on mantra meditation and diverse yogic techniques including breathing exercises and chanting incantations or mantras derived from esoteric and religious texts.

99

Poetic Inspiration

No matter how many times I write,
I always feel the greatest delight.
The ideas might be redundant and words might not flow,
Then to Nature I must bow.
Nature is the greatest manifestation of my Mother,
Having such a benefactor why should I suffer?
Limitless is my Lord but the language has limitations,
Words are after all even at best imitations.
Once a theme arises in my heart,
The rest arranges like a game of darts.
In perfect order I must say,
I think I am a natural if there has ever been one till day.

100

Traversing the Mind

While traversing the lane of the mind,
Various travails I left behind.
Some are still to come my way,
They might be strong but they shall obey;
All my dictates or else I must slay.
These negative thought patterns are your own creation,
Since you are the progenitor in your hands lies their devastation.
Fear not the mind it is just a tool,
But one which can make you the greatest fool.
Do not allow it to ever control your life,
Tame it and conquer life's every strife.

101

Divine Wine

Once I met a man at the tavern,
I offered him to have a sip of my 'wine'.
Inebriated he fell and started to gurgle,
Now I was in the midst of great trouble.
Such was the effect on the poor soul,
He thanked me with his heart as if he had reached life's ultimate goal.
Crying profusely he said "Few are the intoxicants I have not tried.
Yet for this wine of Love my heart always cried."
Not knowing the magic wand of my hands,
I refused to give another a taste for Allah for me had other plans.

102

Saga of the Master

I play with words,
The ancients played with swords.
Expansion was the goal then and so it is today,
Kings had royal empires while literary ones were left for the poets of the day.
Today we have a global market that we intend to capture,
More than selling, sharing is what drives me to rapture.
May the Cosmic One shower His grace on me,
And bless me by showering His unconditional beyond all degree.
This journey started with two when the Master asked me to stay behind,
Till we meet in the physical I shall to a home be confined.
And later become a minstrel of the Divine,
The one who only sings for the pleasure of the Lord and leaves everything behind.

103

The Enigma of Love

Love is all inclusive and the same can never be said about lust,
Love unites the souls while lust reduces vitality to dust.
To admire or desire a body of flesh and blood,
Is a popular trend today for the so called studs.
Popularity and attention I have received in plenty,
Yet self-centred are the motives for gratification.
Wisdom dawns when you differentiate between all kinds of emotions,
And know the sensory impulse is its prime motivation.
Loving God is indeed abstract but by the Grace of the Spiritual Master it is acquired,
Revel all you want in the love of the world but one day the Beloved shall be required.

104

Entreaty to the Mother

Though I am a sinner past redemption,
Yet Thou are my sole hope great beyond mention.
From my mind has dissolved all tensions,
I now seek Divine Intervention.
The enemies are many in number,
Yet they can be vanquished down under.
The One who is my Shadow and Love,
Reigns on earth as well as in Heaven above.
What fear can one have when You are near,
You reside in my heart and there is none as You dear.

105

The Cosmic Illusion

God is One and yet He appears in name and form,
Though transcending each and every societal norm.
For the Absolute there is no separate Truth,
It is One and yet distinct in its various roots.
The riddle of the Lord can never be solved,
I dare to glorify the Almighty but hope my transgressions be absolved.
For I certainly know not what I do,
Though I have eloquence yet am not different from any of you.
The Truth does not require publicity it is evident itself,
Once you attain a glimpse of It you will never be your former self.
The spark will certainly ignite violent flames,
Burning ignorance in a moment and ending Maya's game.

106

Death and its Trappings

Death is the star which we wish to destroy,
Yet it is beyond the control of you and I.
One lives as if the span would extend to eternity,
Yet nothing could be a greater lie than its finality.
It does not accept bribes or cheques in its favour,
This is the bitter pill that you must have to savour.
Each moment is the gift of the Supreme Divine,
So be careful in utilising the remaining time.
Death is the ultimate equaliser depicting life's Vanity Fair,
Death though a destination is not the end I swear.

107

Eternal Consciousness

When Death comes to me I shall greet it with open arms,
For I know it is formidable yet it can never cause me any harm.
Death is the greatest myth as I said earlier in a verse,
Yet it is a portal to dimensions which we never physically traversed.
Life is eternal as consciousness never ends,
And never in front of death does life ever bend.
For there is only life after life,
Some may consider it good while the rest may be filled with strife.
Yet I declare to all and sundry that life is not a combination of chemicals mundane,
But immaculate consciousness of the soul which eternally remains.

108

Farewell

Like all things good my book should also come to an end,
But my readers I do not take lightly they are my best friends.
I have strung the Rosary this time with Divine Love,
My next work shall be in prose meddling with the One up above.
It has been a joy to write and I hope you loved to read,
This is a work of Love transcending each and every creed.
It was conceived in Love Divine,
The outpourings refer to experiences beyond the scope of time.
I am always there to serve and care,
With God as my witness I firmly declare that I will always be there;
For my audience who give me their valuable time and buy my book,
I welcome all queries and doubts coming from each and every nook.